Reducing the Drama in Business Relationships

Understanding Why People Act the Way They Do

Alison Henderson

First Edition, 2015

Moving Image Consulting
www.MovingImageConsulting.com

Reducing the Drama in Business Relationships

Understanding Why People Act the Way They Do

Alison Henderson

Table of Contents

Introduction

As often happens, my career path has not been a linear one. I have multiple degrees in theater and directing, seeking life in front or behind the curtain. Needing those "day jobs" to support my theater aspirations has introduced me to a variety of businesses. Why, I wondered, is there more drama in my office than there is on my stage?

One of my post-graduate trainings was the Graduate Laban Certificate in Movement Analysis from Columbia College Chicago. I immediately used Laban's work with actors, but felt there was more I could do. Rudolf Laban wrote, "Man moves to satisfy a need." This statement haunted and inspired me. What was the need I was feeling which required fulfilment? What was my move to satisfaction? The answer was in Warren Lamb's application of Laban's work called Movement Pattern Analysis (MPA).

I am proud to be one of the twenty-two Certified Movement Pattern Analysts in the world. This unique specialty is the answer to how I can blend my theatre talents in observing behavior with an accurate and highly effective tool for the entrepreneur and business leader. Every time I speak about my MPA consulting work, I am asked if I have a book. Now my practical book on utilizing the decision-making process for business is here for you.

As a theater director and acting coach, I examine what motivates characters to take action. Using character motivation allows me to stage efficiently and to clarify character relationships. The same applies to business. Identifying what motivates you and your employees benefits your organization by increasing efficiency of teams and clarifying communication to reach company goals. Morale is boosted and company culture improves.

Shakespeare nailed it when he said, "There is nothing either good or bad but thinking makes it so." Approaches to decision-making are not good or bad until a colleague reacts based on his own thought processes. By the end of this book, you will have determined some of your decision-making preferences and how to remain objective in your relationships with others. You will understand your inherent action motivations which impact your performance under the bright lights of your business stage.

Inherent action motivations are key to business strategy, efficiency, and productivity because:

- *Inherent action motivations are specific to each individual based on decision-making preferences.*
- *Inherent action motivations are consistent regardless of the subject of the decision.*
- *Inherent action motivations are key to successful client and employee communication.*

The name Moving Image Consulting was conceived because the decision-making process fuels our perceptions and the images we have of ourselves and others. These images move us to alter our behavior and impact our relationships. Moving Image Consulting uses MPA Profiling to create a powerful, goal-driven business strategy. Verbal and non-verbal communication are combined for greatest impact on company messaging, effective presentations, increased sales, and workforce communication.

Return the book if you anticipated learning Movement Pattern Analysis. This book does not teach how to assess an individual's decision-making process using Movement Pattern Analysis. Only certified trainers approved by the Warren Lamb Trust can teach the observation skills used by Movement Pattern Analysts for Decision-Making Profiles.

This book is a guide to intrinsic motivations relating to specific decision-making processes. The guide provides tools for entrepreneurs and business team leaders, but does not replace the Movement Pattern Analysis Profile. There are nuances that will not be discussed in this book because of the individualized nature of each profile.

Movement Pattern Analysis and its theories are not psychology or therapy. I am not a therapist. The examples and discussions in the book are from my training and experience.

The vocabulary I use is consistent with the Movement Pattern Analysis industry. Other terms which evolved through my work with clients are clearly designated.

This book would be incomplete without a short history of Movement Pattern Analysis (MPA) and recognition of its founder Warren Lamb. Movement Pattern Analysis was developed by Warren Lamb (1923-2014) who worked closely with movement theorist Rudolf Laban (1879-1958). While consulting in factories after WWII, Lamb used the movement observation theory of Laban to begin identifying recurring patterns of movement and their significance in a manager's decision-making process. While working in his own consultant firm, Lamb furthered his initial research, successfully applying observation methodology to a decision-making framework.

Lamb's assessment technique is being used by consultants around the world. More than 30,000 individuals have been assessed with MPA and more than 400 companies have used this tool for executive training, applicant assessment, team building, and improved communication skills. The process has been validated by studies at Harvard, Brown, and the U.S. Naval War College. The Warren Lamb Trust is the certification body of Movement Pattern Analysts and oversees periodic consultant examinations to maintain industry standards. Moving Image analysts are members of The Warren

Lamb Trust Registry. Visit www.warrenlambtrust.org for more information.

For exponential growth and even greater understanding, I encourage you to engage a Movement Pattern Analyst for an individual profile.

Alison Henderson

Part I
Explanation of the Motivation to Act

"There's place and means for every man alive."
William Shakespeare, *All's Well That Ends Well*

CHAPTER 1
Introduction to
Movement Pattern Analysis

Movement Pattern Analysis (MPA) is a system for recognizing the decision-making process of individuals through their unique movement patterns. Everyone has a subconscious body movement signature which is why we can recognize someone walking toward us from far away before we can see his face. Movement characteristics give comedians their material from which to create impersonations of politicians and celebrities.

Movement Pattern Analysts are trained to observe unique movement characteristics and equate them to different mental processes used when actively making a decision. Patterns of these specific movement characteristics are recorded by an analyst during the duration of a face-to-face interview. Analysts do not use gestural behavior for their data. They are observing movement patterns during very brief moments in time when an individual's entire body is involved in a process of physical change. The data recorded is calculated into the amount of time an individual will spend on any cognitive process during the decision-making process.

Just as with other leadership or work-style assessments, understanding how data is gathered is less important than the results. Comprehending which movement characteristic correlates to which thought process is immaterial to how the resulting leadership and communication style impacts your business. The brilliance of this technique is its accuracy. Since an individual's report is based on subconscious behavioral observations, the assessment cannot be faked. An individual will not be able to control his subconscious movements for the entire duration of an interview. Since the individual does not know what movements have meaning, he is unable to skew results toward a report he feels his company desires.

Reducing the Drama in Business Relationships concentrates on the results from the Movement Pattern Analysis Profile and how to apply these results to benefit your business.

Whether you are a solo entrepreneur or the leader of a Fortune 500 company:

- *You interact with others and need to know how to better motivate them.*
- *You create project teams and are required to navigate meetings for maximum efficiency.*
- *You hire employees and consultants and must increase retention.*

Reducing the Drama in Business Relationships will support you in all these objectives, but only if you implement the tools into your business. Take the time to complete the exercise. It is vital to your success.

If you are a business of one, you are the leader or facilitator in all of the examples in the book. Think of potential or current clients as the individuals on your team. Consultants you hire equate to your employees. Everything in the book relates to you and your business. You will be able to grow your team utilizing the wisdom in this book.

Before reading, fill out the following pages. These answers will be referenced several times in the book. By taking a few minutes now to give thoughtful and thorough answers, you will understand the concepts better and will have an easier and faster time improving your business. Resist the urge to skip past the exercise now and complete it after you continue reading and need to reference the information. The less you know about Movement Pattern Analysis and the decision-making process while completing your answers, the better.

If you already have your Movement Pattern Analysis Profile, turn to Chapter 2 and do not complete the following exercise.

Exercise: What Would You Do?

Imagine that the following projects or tasks were real needs of your company. Write out the order of the steps you would use and why you would do each step. If there is a project in your business similar to the list below, feel free to change the object of the task to fit your situation. For example, #1 can be altered to purchasing software, a building or a security system; #2 can be revising your website, brochure or employee handbook; #3 can be redesigning landscape, a logo or product…

1. Purchasing a new computer system

My process step by step and why:

_____

_____

_____

_____

_____

_____

_____

_____

_____

_____

_____

_____

_____

_____

2. Revising your board by-laws and mission statement

My process step by step and why:

_____

_____

_____

_____

_____

_____

_____

_____

_____

_____

_____

_____

_____

_____

_____

_____

_____

3. Redesigning your office

My process step by step and why:

_____

_____

_____

_____

_____

_____

_____

_____

_____

_____

_____

_____

_____

_____

_____

_____

4. Mentoring a new-hire

My process step by step and why:

_____

_____

_____

_____

_____

_____

_____

_____

_____

_____

_____

_____

_____

_____

_____

_____

_____

5. Organizing a quarterly retreat

My process step by step and why:

_____

_____

_____

_____

_____

_____

_____

_____

_____

_____

_____

_____

_____

_____

_____

CHAPTER 2
The Motivation to Act—
Stages of Decision-Making and Action Motivations

If you did not read and complete the previous exercise, turn back to finish the exercise before continuing. Do not skip this step.

Each individual has a unique decision-making process. It is vital to keep in mind that concepts in this book are introduced in an order that does not necessarily match the order in which you and your colleagues process through a decision.

Stages of Decision-Making and Action Motivations Overview

What is the thought process when making a decision? Movement Pattern Analysts divide the process of decision-making into six cognitive processes termed Action Motivations. Each person progresses through the six Action Motivations in his own unique way, spending a different amount of time in each process. While you won't be able to figure out the fine nuances like an analyst, this book utilizes behavioral and verbal clues you can use until an analyst is hired.

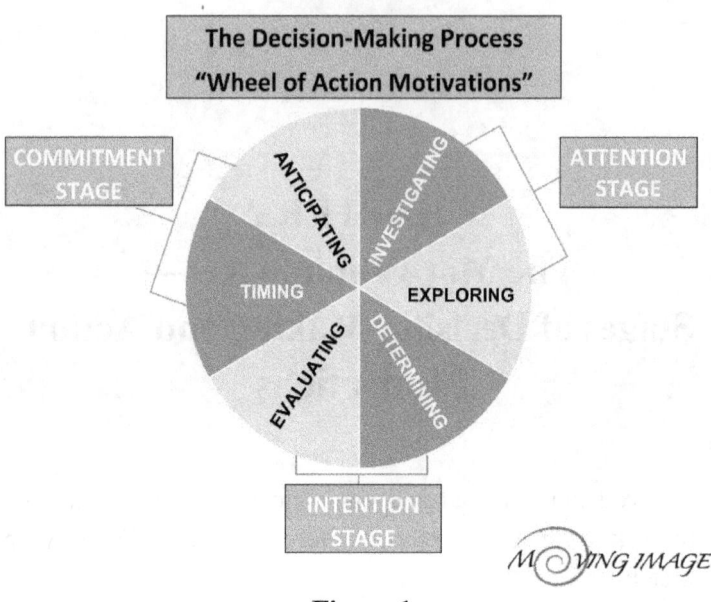

Figure 1

As seen in Figure 1, the Decision-Making Process contains three overall stages to making a decision; Attention, Intention and Commitment, with two Action Motivations per stage. The Attention Stage encompasses Exploring and Investigating; the Intention Stage contains Evaluating and Determining; and the Commitment Stage comprises Anticipating and Timing. Since there is no stage or approach that is better than any other, the processes are put into a framework called the Motivation to Act. To assist clients in comprehending their preferences, I transfer this framework into what I term a "Wheel of Action Motivations." Individuals may start their decision-making process anywhere on the Wheel and move to any other area. There is no "correct" order to making a decision. Analysts calculate percentages for each Action Motivation which creates an individualized Wheel for each client. Typically, individuals process through a decision from the greatest magnitude to the least. An example of a complete Wheel of Action Motivations is at the end of chapter six.

Information Gathering: The Attention Stage

The name **Attention Stage** is derived from bringing attention to a decision. What do I need to know to make and implement this decision? The Attention Stage is often assumed to be the first stage; however, individuals may gather their information after the Intention Stage or Commitment Stage. Looking broadly into options and alternatives for action is called **Exploring**; and drilling down deeply into just one option to gather as much information as possible is called **Investigating**. Managers in this stage lead by innovation and method. Individuals who spend the most time in Attention, I call "Researchers."

Making a Decision: The Intention Stage

The name **Intention Stage** originates from becoming intent about the decision. Why does this decision matter and how important is it to me? The Intention Stage will often occur as a bridge between the Attention Stage and the Commitment Stage; however, some people do start their decision-making process in Intention. Prioritizing, weighing importance, and assigning value to the decision is called **Evaluating**; and standing firm, building resolve, and resisting opposition is called **Determining**. Mangers in this stage lead by realism and mission. A course of action is settled on in this stage. Individuals predominant in Intention, I term "Judges."

Taking Action: The Commitment Stage

The name **Commitment Stage** results from committing to the decision. Not always the last stage, implementing by planning long term and foreseeing consequences is called **Anticipating**; and seizing short-term opportunities to take action is called **Timing**. Managers in this stage lead by vision and opportunism. There is no reversing the decision at this point. Individuals prevalent in Commitment, I call "Action Heroes."

In the next chapters, the characteristics of each type of decision-maker and their intrinsic motivations will be discussed.

CHAPTER 3
The Motivation to Act—Characteristics of the Three, Overarching Types of Decision-Makers

Keep in mind that the following characteristics for each type of decision-maker are broad and generalized. No person can be highly motivated in every stage because the total time spent processing equals 100%. Every person motivated for the same particular stage will be slightly different from one another. Each part of the Decision-Making Profile affects the other parts by intensifying or diluting how characteristics are perceived. Preferences for one process over another create the decision-making process and corresponding decision-making personality for that individual.

The descriptions and examples in this chapter are for an individual with strong motivation to complete the processes specific to that stage of decision-making. Every person is capable of and does process through all six action motivations; however, individuals are strongly motivated to process in some and barely motivated in others.

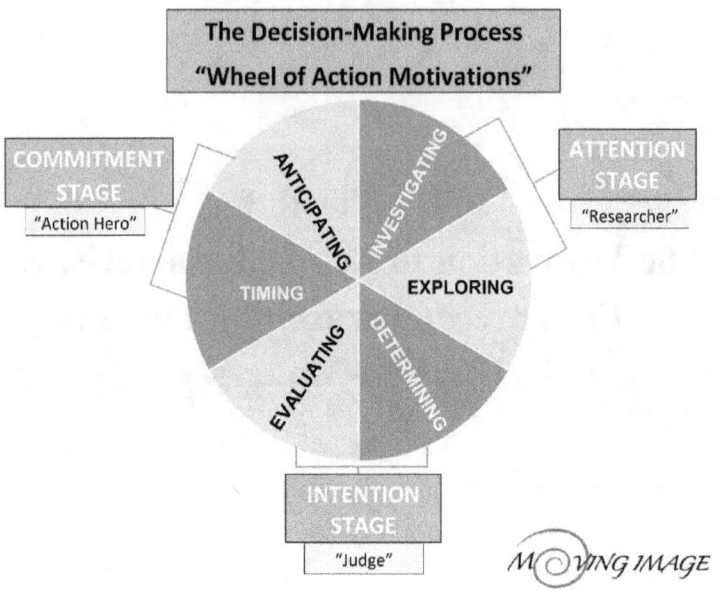

Figure 2

"Researchers": The Attention Stage

Since Researchers spend most of their time finding information in breadth and in depth, information motivates. For those inclined to prefer options (Exploring), they will be inspired, even distracted, by "the next great thing." They may have difficulty making a decision to purchase something because of the allure of the next model or the feeling that more choices remain to be discovered. Similarly, the Researcher who likes more detail (Investigating), may keep delving deeper and deeper into minute information about a subject regardless of relevance. Researchers will slow down a process, thinking there is more to find before proceeding.

How to Identify a Researcher:

Researchers ask detailed questions about information. They will brainstorm for the group, continually finding more options and asking, "What about _____?" The Researcher will be lost in the world of the internet because there are endless pages of "hits" and videos to watch. Being well-prepared is a must for the Researcher.

Misconceptions about Researchers:
- **Researchers are organized.** Even though Researchers require much information and preparedness, the notes and information may not be neat and tidy.
- **Researchers do not make mistakes.** Information and ideas do not equate to being error-free whether it be the information itself or how it is delivered. For example, Researchers may have spelling and grammatical errors even though details are important to them.
- **Researchers are procrastinators.** They are not delaying action with ill intentions, they simply have a difficult time knowing when they have enough information.

An Example of a Researcher Opening a New Bank Account:

A Researcher will go on-line to gather information about at least three different banks. Still lacking enough information, he might call or visit each bank to ask specific questions about what services are offered to businesses, such as fees, hours, on-line banking, loans, etc. At the end of Attending to the decision, the Researcher will have amassed a large quantity of information about multiple banks. The Researcher must feel he has sufficient knowledge to move to another decision-making stage.

"Judges": The Intention Stage

Since Judges evaluate a potential decision and build resolve to stand firm in that decision, value and mission motivates. For those who lead with prioritizing information

(Evaluating), being realistic about the decision is important. For those who enjoy building resolve and standing firm in their convictions (Determining), obstacles and push-back are energizing. Judges may stall progress by either wanting more clarity than is warranted or by being inflexible.

How to Identify a Judge:
Judges ask "why" questions. "Why is this important to us? Why should I care about this? Why is this better than something else?" The Judge will need clarity of value in black and white. The Judge will hold his ground and be steadfast in his resolve. The Judge may need to ask others for their opinion and have consensus before moving forward.

Misconceptions about Judges:
- **Judges are narrow-minded.** Due to their need for clarity and their focus on the positive and negative for the decision, Judges are often accused of being narrow-minded. They may be open to more choices; however, each choice will be subject to the same evaluative process.
- **Judges are always correct.** Since they stand firm in their opinions and do not give in easily, others may tend to accept the Judge as correct despite information to the contrary.
- **Judges are "kill-joys."** The need for realism can cause Judges to voice comments or strike down ideas which deflate exuberance or morale.

An Example of a Judge Opening a New Bank Account:
The Judge will have in his mind what is most important when banking and will seek out only the information that can be classified and prioritized to his criteria. Location may be more important than teller hours; free business checking may

trump interest rates; and the number of ATMs across the country may be at the top. The Judge may ask the opinion of bank customers or seek on-line review sites before making up his mind. If the Judge feels the bank is not offering an important requirement, he will push to obtain it and won't be afraid to walk away if the bank does not acquiesce to his demands.

"Action Heroes": The Commitment Stage

Since Action Heroes prefer to be involved in implementation, opportunities motivate. For those who gravitate to long-term planning (Anticipating), setting goals and fitting action into established systems are stimulating. For those who seize opportunity and change pace in the short-term (Timing), finding the right moment to act and project turn-over are energizing. The Action Hero may "leap in" before having information or support to complete the task. Action Heroes may worry about potential consequences they foresee with the project. Action Heroes may also be competitive.

How to Identify an Action Hero:

Action Heroes ask "how" and "when" questions. "How are we going to accomplish this? How does this fit into our short and long term plans? When is the deadline?" They may be concerned with the timeline and who is going to do what to accomplish the task. Action Heroes excel at changing the pace of implementation and adapting to in-the-moment changes. Oftentimes, Action Heroes are quicker to raise their hand and volunteer to take action or lead the charge. Action heroes will regularly push others who want to research or deliberate, and they usually accuse others of taking too long to finalize a decision.

Misconceptions about Action Heroes:

- **Action Heroes are good team leaders.** Team assembly and delegation are not linked to action motivation. While the Action Hero is sometimes better at team assembly and delegation, he may take charge to the point of not delegating and doing everything himself.
- **Action Heroes are sloppy.** Precision, or lack thereof, is not tied to action motivation. There are just as many neat Action Heroes as there are messy Action Heroes.
- **Action Heroes work quickly.** While the Action Hero may decide quickly to take action, not all Action Heroes work at an accelerated pace. Some individuals have the habit of implementing projects slowly. Action Heroes are adept at moving at either pace.

An Example of an Action Hero Opening a New Bank Account:

The Action Hero will be motivated to choose a bank that has a special on interest rates or free checking for a limited time because he feels the pressure to "act now." He may also seize an opportunity that fits into a current system or a future plan. If a bank location is on his route to work or he uses the bank for personal business, he will be more likely to choose it because the bank fits into his routine. If the long range goal of his business is rapid expansion, he will be motivated to choose a bank that will accommodate growth so he doesn't have to change banks again. He may also choose the bank with the least paperwork and the fastest sign-up so he can move on to something else.

CHAPTER 4
The Motivation to Act—
Perspective/Assertion Approaches in
Each Stage of Decision-Making

There are two ways to approach each stage of decision-making—the **Perspective Approach** and the **Assertive Approach**.

The *Perspective Approach* is a style in which the individual assesses the "big picture" and overall context of the initiative and creates a strategic position from which to take action. The Perspective individual uses little physical effort to accomplish initiatives. Others do not readily observe the individual "working hard" because most of the Perspective Approach involves mental activity over physical activity. Perspective Action Motivations are Exploring, Evaluating, and Anticipating. (See Figure 3.)

The *Assertive Approach* is a style in which the individual exerts dynamic energy on the environment. The Assertive individual applies obvious effort to accomplish initiatives. Others can observe the individual "working hard" at his decision due to the physical effort he expends. The Assertive Action Motivations are Investigating, Determining, and Timing. (See Figure 4.)

Alison Henderson

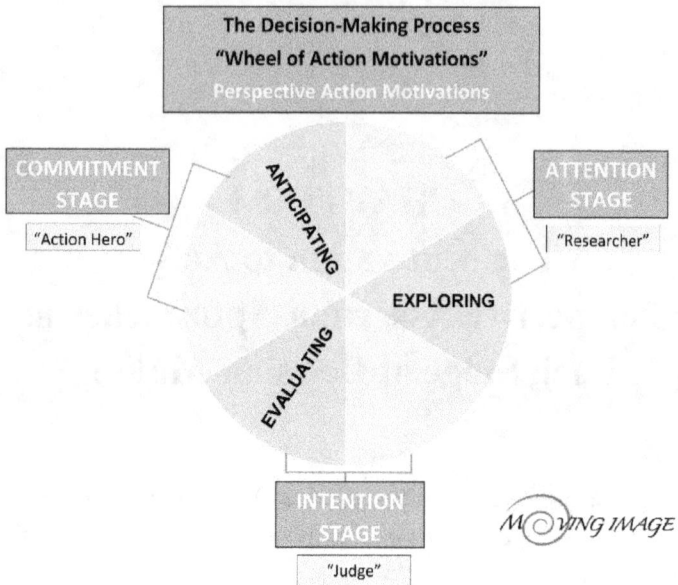

Figure 3: Perspective Action Motivations

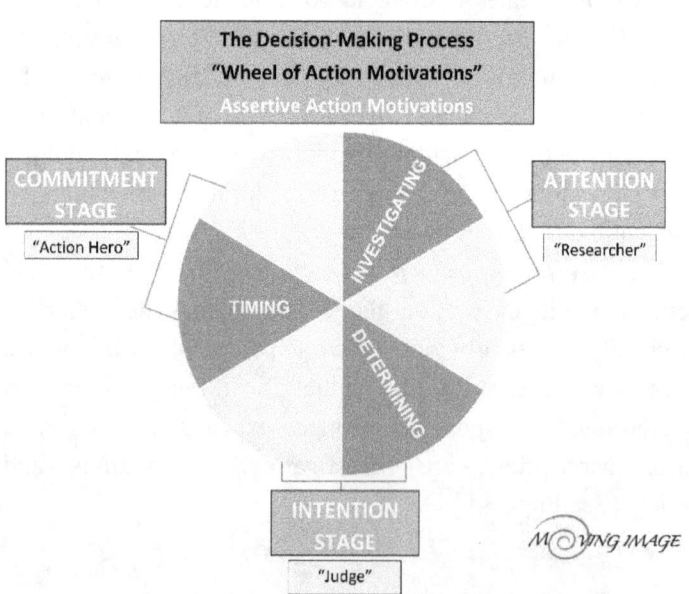

Figure 4: Assertive Action Motivations

The sum of the percentages of the three Perspective Motivations and the sum of the percentages of the three Assertive Motivations create the Perspective/Assertion Ratio. Differences in how an individual approaches a decision are noticed by others and color perception. The Perspective/Assertion ratio has direct influence on how an individual is motivated and how colleagues relate to him.

The ratio is a slightly more difficult aspect of the profile to explain. The difference becomes clear when considering the actions taken in each approach. Researchers will either brainstorm options with little physical effort (Exploring) or will seek information in books with obvious effort expended to find sources and read (Investigating). Judges will either list priorities and figure out personal value with little physical involvement (Evaluating) or will resist outside pressure and push through obstacles requiring physical effort (Determining). Action Heroes will either fit long-range plans into an existing system with little physical effort (Anticipating) or will seize opportunities, adjust pace, and execute plans displaying physical effort (Timing).

A good illustration of the two styles is the office party. Regardless of the size of party, the perspective-oriented party planner caters the event and uses decorations stored in the office from a previous party. This requires less obvious effort than the assertive-oriented party planner who prepares the food, shops for new decorations, and sets up the room. The Perspective Approach appears effortless to others while the Assertive Approach is seen by all as the planner makes multiple trips to his car and the breakroom refrigerator.

Another example is a company restructuring. The perspective-oriented CEO strategically restricts the budget and resources of a division and slowly pushes opposing leaders out of the company until the division is "starved out" and fails from within with little effort from the CEO. The assertive-oriented CEO will take a more direct approach by closing offices, firing teams, and hiring new personnel with much upheaval and effort.

In both examples, the outcome is the same. The office enjoys the party and the company is overhauled.

These two approaches cause tension in the workplace because individuals squarely in one camp or the other rarely understand each other. Perspective individuals perceive assertive individuals as "workaholics" because they exert so much effort, do not use their resources well, and resist delegation. Assertive individuals think perspective individuals are "lazy" because their work is less effortful, results seem to appear out of thin air, and they may delegate much of their work.

The difference in approaches can become a source of personal anxiety for individuals as they are promoted within an organization. "Worker bee" assertive individuals are often promoted quickly because their work is easily seen and recognized by management. Once at a management level, assertive individuals become unhappy or at a loss because suddenly they are less successful and even criticized in employee reviews. This occurs because the assertive individuals are now being asked to be more perspective in their duties. They are tasked with looking broadly and with a long range view of the organization while delegating the "busy work" for which they were previously praised. Assertive individuals feel like their valued assets no longer apply. The company should work with new managers to transition into their new roles by adapting and finding ways to work within their assertive preferences even when in a more perspective-oriented position.

Low-level perspective individuals, on the other hand, often struggle to be promoted because their work is not easily seen and recognized. These individuals need to make certain they are communicating and showing their work and effort to superiors. Once they have ascended to management positions, they feel they have worked very hard to "rise to their positions" and often hold a grudge against others around them who rose more quickly. However, they should embrace the chance to shine and showcase their vision and foresight for the future.

CHAPTER 5
The Motivation to Act—
Decision Loading

The preceding chapters covered parts of The Motivation to Act which analysts calculate to exact percentages. Also included in the Motivation to Act are overall factors called Decision Loading and Identifying. These factors are more generalized and influence how an individual is perceived by others, and how they will act within their decision-making type.

Decision Loading is an overall factor related to the number of different decision-making processes an individual is comfortable balancing at one time. This is not "multi-tasking" in which an individual simultaneously talks on the phone, types on the computer, and watches dinner in the pan. Decision Loading is processing multiple projects all in various decision-making stages at one time. An example would be a manager simultaneously overseeing the installation of some equipment (Commitment Stage); researching consultants for a leadership training (Attention Stage); and building support across divisions for a company-wide customer relations management system (Intention Stage). While this manager is not physically completing each project at the same time, the projects are occurring concurrently. Decision Loading does not require multiple projects be in different stages. For example, an individual could be researching multiple initiatives all in the Attention Stage.

The Decision Loading factor is given as a number between one and ten corresponding to a general "low," "moderate," or "high" level of loading processes. A high loader will be motivated and comfortable with multiple projects in various stages of development happening all at once (like the manager in the above example). A moderate loader can handle several projects at once, but will have a lower loading limit than his high-loading counterpart. The low loader is stressed by multiple projects and works best sequencing through one project at a time.

Decision Loading does not equate to the length of time an individual will take to complete multiple tasks. The lower loader may still complete four projects in the same amount of time as the higher loader. While the high loader is juggling all projects by working on each a little at a time, the low loader completes a project beginning to end and moves to the next.

Just as perspective individuals and assertive individuals clashed, so too do high loaders and low loaders. The low loader thinks the high loader is taking on too much, whereas the high loader thinks the low loader should be able to take on more. High loading bosses tend to overload their subordinates because they falsely think that everyone can handle many things at once. In contrast, the low loading boss may not be delegating enough to their high loading subordinates who feel bored or less challenged with singular projects.

Loading is an area which can create employee stress, but is one of the easier factors to manage. Upper management should communicate with subordinates to understand how they handle their work load. Do they wish to have more or are they already overwhelmed? If they are feeling overwhelmed, the manager should parse out projects or prioritize a large list so staff understands which project to tackle first, second, etc. as they sequence through. If they will thrive with more projects, increase their assignments. Keep in mind, if employees do not easily separate personal and professional lives, remodeling a house, hosting the extended family for the holiday, or caring for a sick family member will add to their work load.

CHAPTER 6
The Motivation to Act—Identifying

Identifying is the degree to which an individual responds and becomes involved in his immediate environment. As an overall factor, it is also given a score of low, moderate, or high. An individual low in Identifying will not be as involved in the environment around him, whereas a high Identifier will spontaneously respond to changes in his environment, even to the point of distraction.

For example, people high in Identifying cannot resist looking up when someone walks by the door because they are heavily "plugged in" to their environment and notice slight changes. A low identifier may not even be aware when someone walks by or is standing in the doorway waiting to be acknowledged.

High identifiers are often perceived as more caring and interested. They are the individuals who are more likely to ask about the personal lives of employees and to respond with empathy. High identifiers are typically more outwardly emotional and may have a difficult time recognizing when involvement is not desired. By contrast, low identifiers are often perceived as less caring and not interested in others. They are less likely to involve themselves in the personal lives of employees, appear calm, and are less obviously emotional.

Perceptions resulting from Identifying are important in the work place. Water cooler negative conversation can be fueled by a lack of understanding or differences in Identifying. High

Identifying is sometimes perceived as "nosey" or "gossipy." High Identifying managers often becomes falsely accused of micromanaging because they are seen walking around and asking how projects are progressing. Individuals are criticized or labeled as being "too distracted," "emotional," or the one who "panics" and "loses their cool" when a situation is tense. The high identifier will be the person who is upset and running around during a crisis but not necessarily helping the situation. The low identifier in the workplace is perceived as aloof, distant, not caring or connected, and even cold. They are criticized or labeled as "too focused," "icy," or even "unaware." The low identifier will be the person taking control of a crisis with calm and composure.

High Identifying is a desired quality in a receptionist whom you want to be aware when someone enters the office and to give a warm greeting. Low Identifying is a desired quality in the manager who first responds to a crisis and needs some measure of reserve to assess the situation. A balanced, or moderate, level of Identifying with others and the environment is desired in most situations. For example, a mid-level manager should have enough Identifying to relate to his subordinates, but not so much that he cannot remain composed in tense encounters.

If a manager recognizes that he is very high or very low in Identifying, he can take steps to be perceived as more moderate. This will reduce or neutralize negative discussion about his management style. Low identifiers can dissuade undesirable opinions that he is uncaring by sending notes of appreciation to employees or by making a conscious effort to reach out to several subordinates a day. More frequent walks around the office or casual lunch offers will also take off the chill. High identifiers can combat their urges to be involved and thereby stave off "nosey" labels by closing their office door or wearing ear phones to drown out environmental distractions like phones ringing or the bell on the elevator. They should cut down on the number of walks around the office.

This concludes the explanation of The Motivation to Act. An example of a client Wheel of Action Motivations follows with a brief description.

Example:

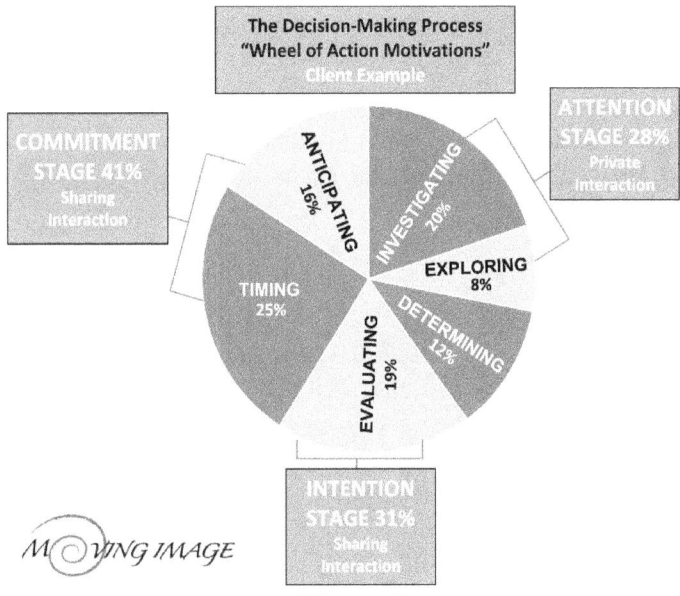

Figure 5

Perspective/Assertion Ratio: 43%/57%
Decision Loading: 7 (moderately high)
Identifying: High

Others will be see this individual hard at work on his projects (57% Assertion). He will be successful balancing multiple projects at a time but should be aware of his limits (Decision Loading, 7). He will be highly aware of changes in his environment and will react spontaneously

This individual is an Action Hero with an opportunistic leadership style who is highly motivated to seize opportunities which fit into his long range goals (Commitment, 41%). He has an adequate amount of Judge in his profile ensuring his initiatives are a good fit for the company and will persist through completion (Intention, 31%). The individual will take on Researcher qualities by seeking plenty of information to support his actions, but will often miss alternatives and should seek out others on his team who are high in Exploring to provide him with options he won't have discovered (Attention, 28%).

This individual will catalyze others to plan and decide a course of action (Sharing Commitment and Intention), but will prefer to report information and will need to be asked for it (Private Attention).

CHAPTER 7
Your Decision-Making Type

Before continuing to Part II, you need to assess your decision-making type.

Assessing your decision-making type is complicated because the purpose of the Movement Pattern Analysis Profile is to provide individuals with a completely objective view of how they make decisions without personal or colleague bias. Movement Pattern Analysts share a goal of eliminating false results which occur during traditional psychometric leadership style tests or personality testing where people try to guess the "right" test answer or create a desired result. Self-evaluation of work style is influenced by many outside forces, such as upbringing, mood, work history, and previous review evaluations. Plus, personal and colleague evaluation is influenced by the decision-making patterns of the individual and the perception of their style qualities by others as previously discussed. To remain objective, Movement Pattern Analysts use a live interview process to observe subconscious, intrinsic movement patterns which are linked to the six cognitive processes outlined in Chapter 3.

Therefore, using written language rather than subconscious behavior is counter to the entire Movement Pattern Analysis belief system. Do not despair. An attempt to reduce personal bias is why you were given multiple situations in which to place yourself rather than a series of questions to answer.

While the nuances in your decision-making process can only be accurately determined by a Certified Movement Pattern Analyst, the following information will guide you to make the best evaluation that you can based on your written responses.

Are You More Researcher, Judge, or Action Hero?

Take a few minutes to examine your answers to the tasks from Chapter 2:

1. Purchasing a new computer system
2. Revising your board by-laws and mission statement
3. Redesigning your office
4. Mentoring a new-hire
5. Organizing a quarterly retreat

After reading the Stage and Action Motivation descriptions in the previous chapters, you probably think you have an idea of what you definitely do first with a decision and perhaps what you rarely do during the decision-making process. Some individuals are surprised by an Action Motivation being included on the Wheel indicating they have an extremely low motivation for that process.

Assess your answers for patterns or commonalities in language. Circle or highlight words or steps which repeat in several situations.

Before going further, realize that information gathering of some kind often occurs as a first step because all decisions need information at some point. Take a step back before you automatically label yourself as a Researcher and look specifically for *how* you use the information, *why* you use it, and *when* you gather it. Consider the following as you decide how you typically use information:

Researcher

Do you mention quantity of information needed for the tasks? Do you use words like "know what the options are" or "being prepared"?

Information can be acquired with a "just in case" purpose before a real sense of what is needed is known. The amount of information may never feel complete. Does finding information and details show up throughout your entire answer?

Do you feel there are more paths to explore or something better exists if you can only find it?

Judge

Is your information prioritized? Do you tie your decision to the mission of the company? Do you use words like "importance" or "valuable" or "realistic"?

Information goes straight to lists of positives and negatives or to supporting your case for steadfastness.

Did you re-organize the task list before you started according to which ones you think relate best to you? Did you resist or even skip answering the ones you concluded were not relevant to you?

Action Hero

Does your language jump right to implementation, planning or developing a system with no additional knowledge? Do you use words like "now is the time" or "future plans" or "vision"?

Is information gathering listed at the end of your response or not at all because it will occur after you have started "doing"?

Do you only research enough to complete the task?

Still not certain? Ask yourself: *Do I find it difficult to stop finding out more? Is the internet a black hole for me? Am I easily distracted by more and more discoveries?* If you answer yes to these questions, Researcher is probably a good fit. If not, you may be using the information for specific purposes as a Judge or Action Hero.

If you have jumped straight to thinking you are primarily a Judge, think about *why* and *when* you evaluate. Do you gather all the information in one big mass (Researcher) and then start to prioritize it? Does evaluation occur only after you have begun building something (Action Hero) and are asked why it is being done? True Judges filter all decisions through evaluation of right and wrong or good and bad as their first step. Judges also check the importance of the decision in relation to other factors. In the by-laws and mission task, the Judge will take each point of the document and ask whether it is still *relevant* and whether it is positive for the organization. If information needs to be gathered to answer these questions, he will go back to research *relative* to the *specific* item.

You may have classified yourself as an Action Hero because you think you are always busy and in action. If this is the case for you, think about *how* you are busy and using your time. Are you busy looking up information and checking out all the options like a Researcher? Do you busy yourself with asking others' opinions, reading reviews, and writing pro and con lists like a Judge? Action Heroes will be busy doing the solution to the problem. In the computer system example, all three types may be "busy" visiting the store. The Action Hero is busy *making the purchase* because the great deal ends tomorrow and he doesn't want to lose the *opportunity*. The Judge is busy asking questions about which system is *better*. The Researcher is busy seeking *details* which were not listed during an on-line search.

Not only will your personal diagnosis be influenced by your decision-making process, but your type is also influenced by what others say about you in reviews or face to face. "He's such a hard worker" does not necessarily equate to Action Hero because the comment links to the Assertive Approach. You could also be working hard at information gathering (Researcher) or standing firm (Judge).

Remember that you will visit all areas of the Wheel of Action Motivations. Having a preference for one area suggests that you will begin your decision-making in that stage. Extreme circumstances may cause you to begin outside of your preference. It is working outside of your preference that will make you feel more stressed. Go back to your exercise answers one more time and look for which stage you typically visit second and then last.

Finally, think about the last decision making process you clearly remember. Maybe it was changing jobs or purchasing your car. Was the decision comfortable and fit your process? If so, think about how it was organic to your process. Was the decision uncomfortable to make? If so, how did that decision negate your natural decision-making process? Think through and write down more decisions and how they relate to your specific Wheel on the note pages at the end of the book.

If discerning your own decision-making preferences has made things less clear rather than more, call a Movement Pattern Analyst and be assessed to remove guessing from the process. Each Action Motivation affects the others, which is why the details of a complete, personalized profile are so important.

To implement many of the suggestions to follow, you will need to know whether others on your team or in your office are Researchers, Judges, or Action Heroes. You may have them answer the same hypothetical situations at the start of the book or take notes of your observations during interactions and meetings. Think through who conflicts with others and why.

Now you will discover how to use the Motivation to Act in your business.

Part II
How to Use the Motivation to Act in Your Business

"We know what we are, but know not what we may be."
William Shakespeare, *Hamlet*

CHAPTER 8
The Motivation to Act—
Meeting Efficiency

Conducting meetings efficiently is key for growth in business. Employees value the efficient use of their time. A comprehensive meeting which finishes within the allotted time creates positive morale and heightened momentum. Company reputations reflect their level of organization which includes productive and efficient meetings.

Decision-making preferences of employees directly affect meeting productivity, efficiency, pace, and completion rate. Strategies should be in place to manage decision-making styles and increase efficiency. Depending on the personalities of the team, changing the format of meetings may have to evolve one element at a time rather than implementing a single complete overhaul. Communicate to participants that meeting structure and leadership will be changing. To facilitate the change with less resistance, be transparent about what is not working, apply the change, and include the team in the process by encouraging feedback.

Once you have support from the group to adjust meeting leaders, utilize one or more of the following strategies based on decision-making preferences. One or two will be successful for your office.

Evaluate the purpose of the meeting and choose a corresponding leader. The best meeting facilitator isn't necessarily the person who called the meeting, nor the highest level manager in the room. The usual leader of a meeting may be too involved to be objective and keep the meeting progressing, or he may be too far removed to know if due diligence has occurred. If the meeting will be evaluating a proposal, seeking consensus, or building resolve against opposition, a Judge should lead the discussion. If you are sharing information or brainstorming solutions, a Researcher should be in charge. Likewise, planning implementation, setting up teams, or deciding on a timeline should be led by an Action Hero.

Utilize more than one leader in a meeting. If the agenda moves from Attention (Researcher) to Intention (Judge) to Commitment (Action Hero), switch up the leaders accordingly. This shares the wealth if the meeting is a success and also shares the responsibility if not much is accomplished. This strategy helps prevent meeting sabotages and will naturally change the tempo and keep the focus shifting which will fend off monotony.

The "natural" leader based on decision-making style in the previous two strategies only works if the individual can reign in his preference and move on when necessary. It does the meeting no favors if the leader prevents progress because he is "in the zone." If this occurs, switch up the leader to a different type depending on the purpose of the meeting or agenda item. An Action Hero or Judge will not get caught up in information sharing like a Researcher and will be able to move to another agenda item. In contrast, a Researcher will not be concerned with the minutia of implementation and could lead planning if the Action Hero proves unsuccessful.

Create a meeting with all the same type. Evaluate the meeting's purpose and invite only those who share the corresponding decision-making preference to attend the meeting. Invite Researchers to the inform-the-project meeting; Judges to the evaluate-the-project meeting; and Action Heroes to the plan-the-project meeting. Depending on the size of the organization, this may not be possible. Consider using this strategy to encourage participation across departments or teams. For most success with this strategy, provide notes from previous project meetings, or one representative from previous meetings should present the project status at subsequent meetings.

Change the meeting environment. Another idea for meeting efficiency is changing the environment or site for the meeting based on meeting agenda or decision-style of participants. If the meeting is debating a new sign design, take Judges to visit the sign company or designer's studio. If the meeting is planning an event, meet Action Heroes on site to walk the space and anticipate problems. Creative Researchers may brainstorm best while painting pictures in an art studio or taking photographs in the woods. If taking notes is difficult, use voice-to-text apps to record the discussion and send after the meeting.

For ultimate efficiency success, all of the above strategies need one common person regardless of meeting strategy or leader. This person is the Timer—the most important person in the meeting. The Timer is given the task of watching the clock and informing participants when three to five minutes are left for each topic. Before the meeting, the facilitator should set both the meeting duration and a time limit for each agenda item. Record the time limit next to each agenda item. The Timer must be able to stand strong and reign in individuals who start to monopolize or detour off topic. The Timer should be announced at the outset, giving him permission to interrupt and maintain the schedule. When time is called, the facilitator should either make note in the minutes that the topic needs revisited at the next meeting, or he should assign the item to a team member to continue addressing and complete.

In any strategy, agendas may need to be created and shared earlier than usual for the evaluation process to occur in time to nominate leaders. If you are unsure as to which decision-maker types you have, send the agenda to attendees and ask for volunteers to lead discussions on the various items. Individuals gravitate toward what they like to do based on their decision-making process and will identify themselves in that way. Whoever volunteers to lead the brainstorming is likely a Researcher; the evaluative section of the agenda will catch the attention of the Judge, and the future discussion will draw the Action Hero.

If meetings continue to create frustration by running long or being unproductive...

1. **Make certain you are being realistic about the time allotted for each item.** Be cognizant of the size of the overall project. If the meeting is about a project with a large scope of comprehensive organizational change, even a two-hour meeting will not address much. Short changing topics in the name of efficiency is counterproductive.

2. **Are there too many people in the room?** If some attendees are invited out of courtesy, yet they are stalling or derailing the meeting, encourage them to keep abreast on project progress with meeting minutes and summaries. Invite them only periodically.

3. **Consider the environment.** Are too many distractions preventing focus? Collect cell phones and tablets at the beginning of the meeting and make it known other employees should not interrupt. If necessary, go off site for the meeting.

4. **Are one or two individuals speaking too much?** Announce time limits for all individuals as during a debate and allow the Timer to cut off speakers. A few meetings with cut-offs will promote brevity.

5. **Encourage attendees to stretch their Judge muscles before speaking and evaluate whether the comments are on or off topic.** If off topic, individuals can make a note to raise the point at the end of the meeting or where it is relevant.

Conference Call Meetings

The former meeting strategies are also successful when meeting virtually. Choosing and changing leaders as necessary is still relevant. If there are numerous people on a conference call, make certain it is clear who is leading which section before the meeting begins. Leadership changes should be clearly identified. The leader will need to call specifically on individuals who are not participating. If the conference call service has the capability for individuals to "raise their hands" when they want to speak, the facilitator will be able to manage contributions more easily and lessen overlap and confusion from many voices speaking at once. The Timer will need to verbally call times or use an audible timer to signal speakers to bring discussion to a close.

CHAPTER 9
The Motivation to Act—Hiring

Movement Pattern Analysis has proven very effective at predicting which candidates have a leadership style and communication style which will fit well within the company culture. Turn-over is greatly reduced in the corporations where it is used. For the highest level positions, Analysts are retained during final interviews to observe and provide a report on a candidate's leadership style.

Similar to evaluating the type of meeting, managers should think about the role being filled and the type of decision maker who will be both happy and retained in that position. Using the Wheel of Action Motivations during the hiring process reduces the problem of managers hiring individuals who are too similar in their decision-making styles.

To identify a candidate's decision-making style, create questions specific to the position and the type of decision-maker who will excel in that role.

- **Take clear notes on how questions were answered; what questions the candidate asked; what he reports is most important to him; and why he is changing positions.** It may be difficult to record his exact language. This may be a time for multiple interviewers with one person taking notes.

- **Ask all candidates about the company culture and work environment of past positions.** Was the candidate happy in the environment or did they wish for something different? Some people thrive in an open office and some people prefer to work from home. If your company's environment is radically different from what the applicant has experienced in the past, careful consideration of the discrepancy must be made. Ask the candidate whether the former environment is a reason he is seeking employment with your company.

- **References should be interviewed and descriptions of the candidates noted.** *"Over-prepared or meticulous"* may indicate a Researcher. *"Stubborn or judgmental"* may point to a Judge. *"Quick to action, leaping before looking, or a worrier"* could suggest an Action Hero. Evaluate if the descriptions given by others matched your impression. If not, the individual may have been conducting himself on his best behavior or was coached on his interview answers to respond how you desired.

- **Review notes after the interview in the same way you examined your process with the exercise in part one of the book.** Look for common themes in language which point to a specific type of decision-maker. Retain these notes for reference even after the candidate is hired to facilitate a smooth transition— decreasing the likelihood you will incur the expense of interviewing and training another new employee in the same position several months later.

The following comments provide additional information to help managers in identifying types of decision-makers during the interview:

Researchers will tend to share much information and may continue speaking until interrupted. They may also share stories that seem to have little relevance to the topic. Wanting to be completely prepared for the interview, they will have scoured the company website and will have talked to present employees. Researchers will ask "what" questions.

Researchers will excel in roles where being prepared and supporting a team with information is required. During interviews, listen for detailed information and ask how a candidate would go about gathering information. If alternatives will be desired or creative thinking required, listen for the candidate to outline different paths tried or when he was involved in brainstorming. During the interview, ask applicants to give you options for real situations they will encounter or initiatives currently in development. A resume reflecting different career paths could signal an exploring Researcher who is looking for the right career. Is your company another trial, or has the individual found the career for his interests?

Judges will attend the interview with their priorities already decided and may try to steer the interview to fit their agenda. They will ask "why" questions about the position and will want to understand why this company stands out or should be a fit for them. They may ask for statistics to help them evaluate. Managers will tend to feel like they are being interviewed and must prove the company's worth, rather than the other way around. During negotiations, Judges will not want to give in on what is important to them. Issues like health care, flexible schedules, and bonus plans will be carefully evaluated.

Judges will not be happy if they can't make decisions, prioritize and stand firm. Listen for opinionated, value-driven statements during their interview. Ask candidates to evaluate their past jobs. Note whether or not it seems like they can be flexible with others or if it is their way or no way. Individuals will try to be amenable in the interview process, so it may be difficult to gauge. Listen for superlative language that has little shades of gray.

Action Heroes will want to know the work schedule, future plans for the position, as well as advancement possibilities. They will ask questions about how their position fits into the company and may often comment about the future they envision. Time is on the mind of the Action Hero. He may reference past projects in relation to when they happened. He will want to know what the time schedule is for filling the position and when he can expect to hear back.

Action Heroes value change and opportunities both short and long term. Take note as to how often they changed jobs and why. Were they dissatisfied or bored? They might not have had enough action. If you suspect an Action Hero, ask them about a project they planned and implemented or ask them how they would take action on a project currently progressing with your company.

Finally, review the chapters on Perspective/Assertion Ratio, Decision-Loading and Identifying. Which of these qualities will be important to the position? Will the role require broad view and long range company positioning (Perspective)? Is the ability to handle multiple projects simultaneously (High Loading) more important than decision-making type? Will the individual be in crisis management and must keep cool (Low Identifying)? Add questions in these areas to your interview process.

CHAPTER 10
The Motivation to Act—Team Development and Management

All the information used for hiring in the last chapter can be used for developing teams. For ultimate productivity, Movement Pattern Analysts advise assembling balanced teams. There are many factors that establish balance. For now, evaluate the type of decision-makers you have and do your best to place at least one of each type (Researcher, Judge and Action Hero) on each project team.

A phenomenon to examine briefly is "group think" which occurs when a team does not have balance and members are too similar in their decision-making styles. The team is happy and everything seems to be going well because there is no opposition. Group think often happens when friends go into business together or an entrepreneur begins to hire staff. It is very easy to fall into the trap of creating teams of people who share the same philosophies and opinions because we think we will be happier and stress free. In business, however, it is often the person who is different who brings the most value by opening the team to various possibilities (Researcher), by helping them stand firm in their value (Judge), or by recognizing an opportunity to exploit (Action Hero). Without variety, a team of Researchers will lose momentum by stalling projects in preliminary processes; a team of Judges will struggle to adapt in the face of obstacles; and a team of Action

Heroes will discover their project was missing vital information for success.

If you realize you have an unbalanced team, identify the missing link(s). Think over the process the team gravitates toward. If they gather information to the point they miss opportunities and have a difficult time making a decision and taking action, the team is skewed to Researchers. If they deliberate, prioritize, and spend too much time on the mission of the organization, the team is composed of Judges. Finally, if they jump into action and burn out easily from seizing too many opportunities, the team is comprised of Action Heroes.

Next, fill the missing gaps by either hiring someone using the interviewing tips in the previous chapter, or take the opportunity during promotions and between projects to reassign teams for balance. Be aware, however, that when someone different is inserted into a skewed team, his contribution must be valued and ideas respected. It is easy for teams to ignore the new ideas and make the newest member feel like the "odd man out." If the team does not accept the new member, he will either quit or stop contributing.

If hiring is not financially feasible and there is no one else in the business to shuffle, it is possible to create some balance on the existing team. Remember that everyone can and does execute all six decision-making processes to some degree. As a manager, tools can be implemented which lead teams to complete processes they are less likely to accomplish otherwise.

For Researchers, be specific about the number of options being sought so they do not become distracted by too many possibilities. Give them a time limit for when the information gathering must be completed. To move them to Intention, ask them to prioritize the material based on relevance to the project. Finally, for Commitment, ask them to recommend and complete a course of action based on the prioritization of information.

For Judges, make certain they gather information for the decision. They are motivated by standing firm, so for this group to give Attention, ask them to gather information to support their position. Be aware, however, that both positives and negatives must be required as it is easy for Judge-heavy teams to only find research in support of their position and to ignore information they find that negates. To facilitate Judges following through to Commitment, ask them to evaluate the best course of action and to take action on their choice.

For teams of Action Heroes, it is essential to establish a system for information gathering, otherwise, they will enter Commitment for a project like a parent assembling a bike with no instructions. Before they are permitted to take action, necessary information (Attention) and a clear "why" (Intention) should be related to an upper manager. If taking action involves a purchase, require these steps before a purchase order will be approved.

For all teams, a reporting process for each stage of decision-making is extremely helpful. A daily log of progress posted in a cloud sharing system where all can see the information, deliberation, and action plan will incorporate motivation for each person. Management can track team progress and be alert to where the project is stalling. For smaller businesses with less hierarchical oversight, enlist a trusted advisor or coach to hold you accountable for each stage of decision-making.

Balanced teams become more crucial when a large cost is involved.

- Researchers may delay a purchase to pursue more information and the cost escalates during the interim. Confirm if the price is too volatile to accept delay.

- Judges may delay a purchase wanting to be 100% positive the brand or company is the correct choice. Motivate Judges to make a decision based on how crucial the purchase is to maintaining business function.
- Action Heroes may encourage a large purchase and benefit from structured delay. Action Heroes suffer "buyers' remorse" by quickly making a large purpose before discovering it will not live up to expectations. Require waiting at least a day before a big purchase. Insist the salesman guarantee to hold the price and take that time to research the product and evaluate its true necessity.

Part III
The Motivation to Interact

"This above all: to thine own self be true."
William Shakespeare, *Hamlet*

Everything in Parts I and II of *Reducing the Drama in Business Relationships* involves only half of the Movement Pattern Analysis Profile—The Motivation to Act. With an understanding of your decision-making style preferences and your overall factors, you are well on your way to improving your business. Part III explains the other half of a Movement Pattern Analysis Profile—**The Motivation to Interact.**

CHAPTER 11
The Motivation to Interact—
Interaction Styles

In addition to Decision-Making Style, Movement Pattern Analysts determine **Interaction Style** of clients because of the influence it exerts on decision-making preferences. Interaction Style represents the individual's collaboration preferences while making decisions. Each person has the capability and desire to both collaborate with others and work independently. There are four Interaction Styles identified by Movement Pattern Analysts named **Sharing**, **Private**, **Neutral,** and **Versatile**. As with Decision-Making Style, a Movement Pattern Analysis Profile is necessary to definitively know Interaction Style, but team dynamics can be improved with an awareness of strategies to manage the various interaction styles.

While influential to Decision-Making Style, there is no Interaction Style that equates to a particular stage. A Researcher, Judge, or Action Hero may be any of the four Interaction Styles in any stage. In other words, an individual may be one Interaction Style in the Attention Stage, a different Interaction Style in the Intention Stage, and a third Interaction Style in the Commitment Stage. An individual may also have the same Interaction Style in two or all three decision-making stages. (See Figure 6 for a graphic illustration.)

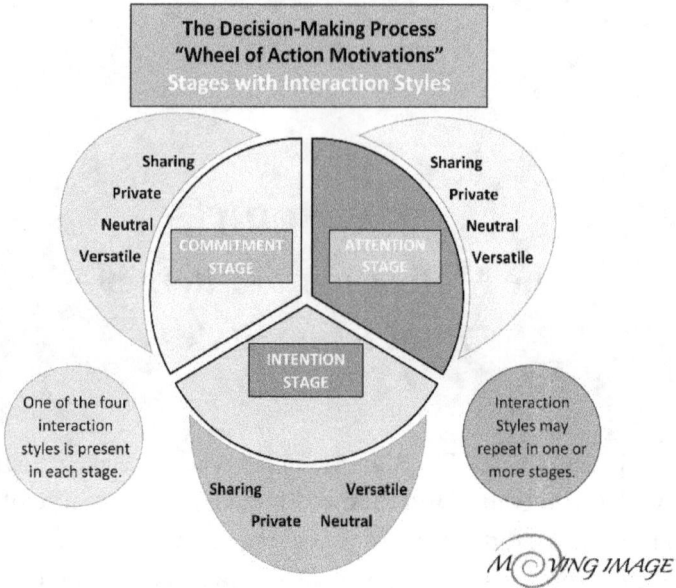

Figure 6

The **Sharing Interaction** style reflects a person's need to actively involve others in a particular stage of the decision-making process. Sharing Interaction is a reciprocal process. The individual needs to both share information **and** receive information back from others. The Sharing individual will not be successful or content in his decision-making process if he has no feedback or interaction with others during the process.

The **Private Interaction** style reflects an individual's need to be independent of the influence of others when involved in a particular stage of the decision-making process. Private Interaction is very much a solo process and the individual must have time to process alone before he will be able to progress through a decision.

Interaction Styles are experienced differently based on the stage. During Attention, Sharing Researchers instigate involvement from others, give information, and alert the group to alternatives. During Intention, Sharing Judges declare purpose and seek to influence and persuade others to share opinions. Sharing judges require consensus from the group before continuing to action. During Commitment, Sharing Action Heroes organize people and coordinate schedules to take action while communicating changes to the pace as they progress. Sharing Action Heroes are aware of consequences to their actions and will be reluctant to begin action if alone.

During Attention, Private Researchers gather information independently, leaving others out of the process. Private Researchers report results and information rather than contribute information to receive a reciprocal response. During Intention, Private Judges build resolve and assess value independently. Private Judges state beliefs and opinions with no concern for agreement. During Commitment, Private Action Heroes seize opportunity and plan for the future independently. Private Action Heroes keep others out of their process.

Neutral Interaction and **Versatile Interaction** are the other two Interaction Styles which are combinations of Sharing and Private. Since these are combinations, an individual appears to others as either Sharing or Private as in the above explanations depending on which style he is favoring in the moment.

Neutral Interaction style reflects a low level of need to either interact in a reciprocal manner or independent manner. A Neutral individual works well with all other types. Since he has no particular desire to interact in one way over another, he adopts the interaction style of those around him. If he is in a team that is working in a Sharing style, he joins in the group. If he is with someone who prefers to work alone, the Neutral person works independently. Since the Neutral person does not feel a need to share, he needs to be asked for his input, otherwise, he will stay silent. Once asked, he is happy to share and will often have a difficult time ending his sharing interaction.

Versatile Interaction style is the opposite of Neutral because the individual feels a strong need to be both Private and Sharing. A Versatile individual, like a Neutral, works well in groups; however, his need to process in both styles makes him unpredictable. A Versatile person will be sharing ideas in the Attention Stage, for example, and will suddenly stop Sharing when the need to be Private takes over. The individual is not aware of changing styles mid-meeting and this sudden "shut down" can be a source of frustration or confusion for others.

Overall style in each stage emerges based on the amount of need the individual feels to interact in either a Sharing or Private manner as Figure 7 illustrates. These styles are vitally important to team balance because these polar opposite ways of collaborating create much friction in the team dynamic.

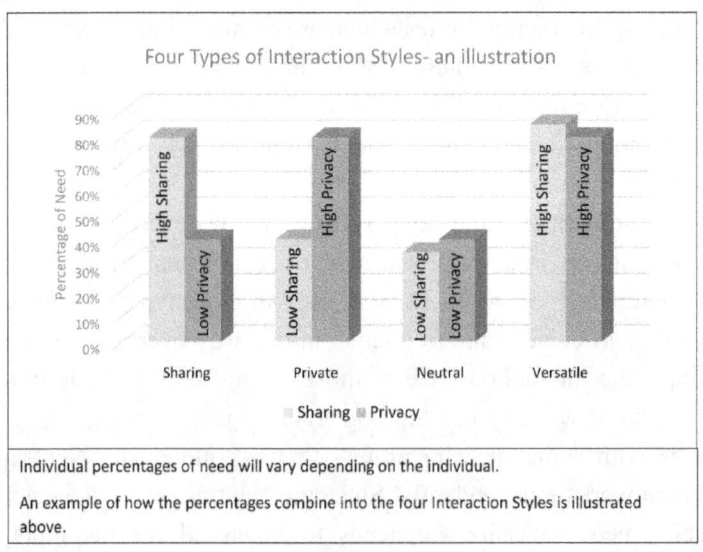

Figure 7

How to Identify a Sharing Individual:

"Sharers" will ask for input from others and may promote meetings to work together. Sharers will be annoyed when their want of interaction is ignored or put off. Sharers will be distracted by social media outlets and will check on what friends are sharing and will respond to them. Sharers will prefer the immediate and interactive nature of texting. Sharers are more likely to start conversations with strangers while waiting in line, typically make friends easily, and will generally be more social.

Misconceptions of Sharers:

- **Sharers are gossips.** Sharers may not have ill intent when rumors are inadvertently begun. Sharers often have difficulty knowing the clear line between what should and should not be shared with others.
- **Sharers need hand holding.** Desire for interaction does not equate to needing help. Sharers are usually more amenable to assistance, but can work independently when necessary. They also may simply desire to relate information and receive feedback without actual assistance.

An example of an individual with Sharing Interaction Style in the Attention Stage tasked with choosing a meeting location:

The Sharer will send out a group e-mail asking for meeting location suggestions. If suggestions do not come in, he will call or text individuals asking for response. If he is still waiting, he will personally interrupt team members at their desks to ask again. Only after feedback will the Sharer be able to progress to choosing and booking a location.

How to Identify a Private Individual:

"Privates" will not seek input from others and will resist meetings that they feel are unnecessary. It is difficult to know where a Private individual stands on an issue and he may take unexpected solo action. Privates will be annoyed when pestered for response, opinion, and collaboration if they deem their response is not warranted. Privates will prefer to give reports to lessen interaction. Privates usually prefer to correspond via e-mail to control when they collaborate. Privates will be comfortable dining, travelling, or living alone and may not have a wide circle of friends.

Misconceptions of Privates:

- **Privates are snooty.** Privates do not mean to appear superior when they are silent or resistant to collaboration. Privates can and will share with others when they feel it is necessary.
- **Privates are sneaky.** Working independently does not equate to dishonesty or withholding information. Private individuals recite information only when it is clearly required. Privates may not give information because they falsely assume other individuals already have the information.

An example of an individual with Private Interaction Style in the Attention Stage tasked with choosing a meeting location:

The Private will conduct an on-line search for meeting location possibilities. He will compile all the information on each location into a report. He will send the report to the team via e-mail, post it in a shared cloud folder, or will pass out printed copies.

How to Identify a Neutral Individual:

"Neutrals" may be difficult to spot because of their ability to blend with others. Neutrals will exhibit traits of both types depending on those around them. A key to picking up on a Neutral is his need to be invited into interaction. A Neutral person will usually not raise his hand in a meeting or will stay on the outskirts of the office social gathering until he is invited to join the meeting or a group.

Misconceptions of Neutrals:

- **Neutrals are shy.** Waiting for the invitation to join and being uncomfortable instigating conversation with others creates a "wallflower" effect for the Neutral person. However, once they are invited, they may not be shy at all.
- **Neutrals are disinterested.** Since Neutrals do not readily share, they may be accused of being uninvolved or not interested in the discussion. To test their interest, ask the Neutral for their opinion or thoughts and see how he responds.

An example of an individual with Neutral Interaction Style in the Attention Stage tasked with choosing a meeting location:

The Neutral individual will begin to choose a meeting location my looking on-line more like the Private individual if no-one is around to dictate a sharing interaction. Once asked to share the information, the Neutral will share his findings.

How to Identify a Versatile Individual:

"Versatiles," like their Neutral colleagues, may be difficult to spot because of their duality of styles. The give-away for Versatile individuals is their ability to switch Sharing on and off. Ask others about those you suspect are Versatile. You will probably hear complaints about never knowing when it is safe to approach them or criticism that they suddenly seem to "check out" during a conversation.

Misconceptions of Versatiles:

- **Versatiles are purposefully disruptive.** Unfortunately, Versatile individuals have very little control or knowledge when they switch styles. It is easier on Versatile people if others accept them as they are and simply verbally draw them back into interaction when they shut down.
- **Versatiles do not care.** Suddenly "turning off" during the project should not be perceived as an intentional snub. The Versatile individual is not conscious of his switch to privacy. He will be confused by accusations that he is disinterested when he "comes back" into a Sharing interaction.

An example of an individual with Versatile Interaction Style in the Attention Stage tasked with choosing a meeting location:

Depending on his needs in the moment, the Versatile individual will either start independently searching or will ask others for suggestions. He will then switch styles at will, asking opinions of others in one minute and turning off to work solo the next. He will share his information when the need arises.

CHAPTER 12
The Impact of Interaction Styles on Business Teams

Awareness of the four Interaction Styles will dissuade much friction in the work place. Even if employees do not label their colleagues as one style over another, increased tolerance will result from sharing the definitions and how they manifest in business situations. When an employee is quick to anger over a miscommunication, step back and analyze if the misunderstanding is caused by a difference in Interaction Style. Impress upon teams that challenges arising from Interaction Style are not intentional. As we are "wired" to process decisions in a certain way, so too are we programmed with habits of interaction.

Managing the Four Interaction Styles:
Due to the way Sharing Interactors and Private Interactors approach the world and the misconceptions they hold about each another, the styles have a large impact on how information is shared within an organization. Different types will be expected to work together despite their preferences. Depending on the composition of the team, the following team dynamics may be observed and will need to be managed.

Sharing and Private styles will be illustrated in their various combinations. Remember that the individual may be Neutral or Versatile in a stage; however, their interaction in the moment will be perceived as one of the two core types, Sharing or Private.

TEAMS:

Privates Mixed with Sharers

The Private individual does not want to share information and will resist the Sharing person's plea for collaboration. Meanwhile, the Sharing individual will feel slighted by the lack of collaboration by the Private person. Processes may be done in duplicate because lack of communication disrupts knowledge and understanding of what the other is doing. To prevent this, duties should be clearly established at the outset of a project. Subsequently, a system for reporting should be created. This could be an update by conference call, a meeting status form, or a posted list of project responsibilities.

Both types should be reminded to be amenable to each other because the friction they feel is just a result of working style preference and not meant to be deliberately irritating.

Privates with Privates

Teams with all Privates will not be very successful unless good reporting systems are in place. Without someone to encourage collaboration, projects may happen very haphazardly with no clear lead or plan. If divisions of a company are all managed by Private individuals, silos in the organization are quickly created with deteriorating efficiency as functions begin to overlap and resources are squandered.

Sharers with Sharers

Teams of all Sharers will become problematic because they encourage collaboration to the point where projects never reach completion. Sharing too much information or requiring complete consensus can stall a project into inaction.

Set hard deadlines for Sharing groups to keep them progressing through a project.

Since every team configuration has its challenges, create and encourage situations in which individuals can collaborate according to their Interaction Style preference. Sharers and Privates will be more willing to participate productively in a team situation or meeting if their Interaction Style needs are met in other ways.

- Encourage Sharers to go out to lunch with a friend or seek out other sharing colleagues during breaks.
- If the business has a social media presence which is managed by an employee, use the Sharing team member to make posts, blogs, etc. This will feed his need to Share, especially if users comment, re-tweet, or tag his posts.
- Give Private employees ample time to work alone whether in the office, from home, or while travelling.
- Praise Privates for posting their information to whatever system is devised. Communicate the value of their contribution and opinions to encourage them to relate.

Be clear about a project's level of importance and sensitivity. A Private person can and will share information, especially if it is in his best interest or the project is labeled as highly important. Similarly, a Sharing person can and will work privately if it is a solo project or something sensitive that should not be shared.

TEAM MEETINGS:

If team meeting design does not incorporate collaboration preferences, meetings can become contentious and unproductive. Private individuals will likely seek to report their information quickly and go back to their desks. Sharing individuals will need to collaborate and deliberate on every point. Private individuals will be frustrated by what they perceive as unproductive chatter (*"Why can't he figure that out after the meeting and come back to us with a decision?"*) and the Sharing individuals will feel the Privates are rude (*"He cut me off and then didn't even contribute to the discussion!"*).

To remedy much meeting contention, utilize the strategies found in the chapter on meeting efficiency and also add the following tips:

- Evaluate the types who will be in the meeting. If there are more sharers, you may need to increase time on each agenda item from the start.
- Ask for each person's contribution to the topic to make sure all Sharers can share, all Privates can report, and all Neutrals are invited to participate.
- Create a funnel for gathering additional ideas or comments after the meeting. Private individuals may think of something of value while independently processing post meeting. Sharers may feel they were cut off and had more to contribute. Versatile individuals may have "submerged" to Private before they had shared everything. Neutral individuals may not have been asked for their contribution. Gathering this information can occur by facilitating a quick conference call follow-up, creating a post meeting form, or walking the office asking for more input.

CHAPTER 13
The Impact of Interaction Styles on Work Environment

Another way to provide for Interaction Style preferences is by examining the work environment and the communication technology in the office.

Open Office

Sharing individuals will prefer an open office configuration where the easy flow of ideas is maximized. In contrast, Private individuals will find working in this environment difficult. If the office is open, set up areas in corners where tables face the wall or have a few cubicles to give some privacy to those who need it. Allow Privates the ability to work part-time from a home office where they can process privately.

Traditional Office

An office divided into rooms with doors will be more amenable to Private employees but will frustrate the Sharer. To create more open spaces, keep doors open and use common areas for open meetings. Allow small groups to easily utilize conference rooms for impromptu meetings. Convert a larger office into a "free" space with tables and chairs where employees can bring laptops, work communally, and share ideas.

Blended Office

Versatile employees will appreciate the flexibility to be both private or share. Neutral colleagues will make any office environment work for them.

Home Office

As more and more individuals work from home, strategies for Interaction Style should be considered. Private individuals will be happy working from home, whereas the Sharing individual may find the lack of interaction challenging. Sharers should schedule in-person meetings or Skype phone calls for their interaction needs. Joining business groups or association committees will also prevent Sharers from feeling isolated.

CHAPTER 14
The Impact of Interaction Style on Written Communication

Just as Interaction Style will impact the work environment, so too will written communication be affected. Length, tone and degree of communication are all influenced.

E-mail

Interaction Style should be considered if the majority of information and action in a company is occurring via e-mail. Once again, friction easily escalates and both parties think the other is to blame. Sharing individuals will feel the need to respond immediately to e-mail and may tend to send out many e-mails as ideas occur. This can be particularly frustrating to a Private individual who either opens his e-mail to an overload from one person or is bothered all day long by the ping or buzz of new mail. In contrast, the Sharing individual will be frustrated by feeling ignored if the Private individual does not quickly respond.

Sharers may create longer e-mails which Privates feel contain too much or unnecessary information. Privates may create succinct responses which are viewed by Sharers as curt or rude.

If opposite styles are on the same project, establish an agreed upon time and number limit for e-mail communication. The Sharer may need to create a list of things to share in one e-mail at the end of the day. This will prevent the situation in which an issue has been resolved during the day rendering early e-mails irrelevant. The Private individual will be highly annoyed from opening, reading and commenting on communication which he discovers is no longer relevant in the last e-mail in the chain. If the Sharer cannot proceed without input, the e-mail should be tagged as important. During crucial times of the project, the Private individual should establish the times of day he will read e-mail and communicate those times to the group.

Texting

Texting can create the same type of problems as e-mails. Sharers should reserve texting for only the most important communications and only if the answers can be short. Private individuals may find texting with Sharers eases friction by creating the immediacy and more communicative/personal feel the Sharer desires.

Neutral and Versatile Interaction Styles with Written Communication

Neutral individuals may not respond to e-mail and texts unless there is "please respond" in the communication. They may think you are simply sharing the information and take it under advisement. Versatile individuals will frustrate the other types by responding in a chain of e-mails or texts only to suddenly go silent and then pop back in. This is often perceived as offensive or uncooperative by those who do not know this is a characteristic of the individual.

Part IV
The Motivation to Act and Interact—
Verbal Communication

"Mind your speech a little lest you should mar your fortunes."
William Shakespeare, *King Lear*

Parts I through III of *Reducing the Drama in Business Relationships* have provided tools for identifying the types of individuals in your business and how to utilize the Motivation to Act and Motivation to Interact primarily for improving team dynamics, meeting efficiency, and office environment. These improvements alone will greatly enhance your business effectiveness, organizational reputation, and bottom line.

Part IV addresses verbal communication. Using verbal language based on decision-making preferences is incredibly effective at improving all areas of your business. Conflicts between employees and with clients arise for many reasons, but as illustrated in the previous sections of the book, disagreements are often tied to the decision-making process. For example, team member A is not motivated to engage in a process which team member B is requiring for the project to progress. The conflict may also be caused by or inflamed by Interaction Style differences. Team member A wants everyone to share in the process and team member B wants everyone to process alone. Moderating conflict is a skill involving practice and should be incorporated by all for greatest positive effect. Understanding how to frame your conversations to ease tension and motivate others is worth the work required to learn the skill.

All the concepts and tools in the previous chapters should be understood and implemented *before* altering verbal communication. Foundational knowledge is required to catalyze the most change with enhanced verbal communication.

CHAPTER 15
Motivational Language

If you are the lead on a project or the manager of employees, it is key to understand what will motivate others. Make sure you have identified your employee's decision-making and interaction preferences. Pepper your conversations with motivating trigger language to capture your colleague's attention and favorably motivate him to complete his task. This prevents putting him on the defensive with a common, knee-jerk reaction like, *"Why don't you have this done?"* Before the conversation turns into blaming others, place any blame on outside circumstances rather than on a person. As soon as others are mentioned, their decision-making styles and resulting conflicts are added to the mix.

Motivating trigger words are in ***bold italicized*** text.

Motivating a Researcher

Use words like ***details***, ***alternatives***, ***options***, ***thoroughness***, ***information***. Ask "what" questions about the project.

Examples:

- "Your ***detailed*** report will be well received. Location ***options*** are just what we need."
- "***What information*** is still needed? I need to alter the meeting agenda."

- *"What facts* have you found about the two products? We are going to make a decision soon."

Motivating a Judge
Use words like *value, opinion, importance, mission, persistence, standing firm, deliberating*. Ask "why" questions about the project.
Examples:
- "I *value* your *opinion* on this decision. It is *important* we keep with the *mission* of the company."
- *"Why do you think* this program is *superior* to the others we have looked into?"
- "I appreciate your *persistence* with the consultants. It is *important* we *don't back down* on our price."

Motivating an Action Hero
Use words like *timeline, process, implementation, future goals, seizing opportunity, pace adjustment, deadline*. Ask "how" and "when" questions about the project.
Examples:
- "The *timing* of *implementation* on this project is crucial to *future* success. *When* you recognize an *opportunity* for *action*, let me know."
- *"When* do you *foresee* this project will reach completion? Do we need to *adjust our pace* to meet our *deadline*?"
- *"How* will we give the presentation? Is the *plan* to use a white board, slides, or video?"

The verbal technique in the above examples seems very simple. However, using these triggers is much more difficult to employ in the moment. It will take practice because you will be working against your own decision-making style preferences unless you share the same type with your coworker. If you are a Researcher, your habit will be to use language like the words in the Motivating a Researcher section above because you will respond to those same language triggers. This is why individuals with similar processing understand each other so well. They literally "speak the same language." When conversing with someone with opposite preferences, you will need to work harder to alter your language.

Persuasion is similar to motivation, but when persuading colleagues, they usually are not already on your side of the issue or you may be convincing them to do something outside of their decision-making preference. You can still use the motivational language tips, but the art will be making it feel like the colleague is doing what he is good at or likes to do while he is really functioning in a different process. Verbal persuasion is similar to the technique in chapter nine encouraging teams to progress to different stages of decision-making by giving specific tasks. Rather than group assignments, verbal persuasion mixes specific trigger language of the desired stage with motivational language in the individual's preferred stage. Each persuasion begins with praise to encourage openness to what you have to say and to bring them closer to your side from the start.

Persuading a Researcher to Perform Like a Judge
(Researcher language is *italicized*, Judge language is **bold**.)
- Begin with praise in the preferred stage: "The *details* and *options* you have found are so helpful. I don't want any of it to go unnoticed."
- Continue with mixing trigger language for the new task: "It will be **clearer** for the team to see the list **prioritized**. Please **categorize** the *information* into **positives** and **negatives** for each *option*."

Persuading a Researcher to Perform Like an Action Hero (Researcher language is *italicized*, Action Hero language is **bold**.)

- Begin with praise in the preferred stage: "The *details* and *options* you have found are so helpful. I don't want any of it to go to waste."
- Continue with mixing trigger language for the new task: "We will be **moving forward** with **implementing** the project **soon**. Please arrange the *information* into **beginning, middle, and end** steps for the team with the **time** you **anticipate** it will take to do each section."

Persuading a Judge to Perform Like a Researcher (Judge language is *italicized*, Researcher language is **bold**.)

- Begin with praise in the preferred stage: "Thank you for *offering your opinion* and *clarifying* for us the *importance* of this project."
- Continue with mixing trigger language for the new task: "In order for us to *stand firm* when questioned, we need **information** and **research** to back our *position*. Please take each *point from the list* and find **supporting information**."

Persuading a Judge to Perform Like an Action Hero (Judge language is *italicized*, Action Hero language is **bold**.)

- Begin with praise in the preferred stage: "Thank you for *clarifying* the *importance* of this project."
- Continue with mixing trigger language for the new task: "To make certain the **implementation** of the project proceeds smoothly, please create an **action plan** of project directions with *why* each step is *important*."

Persuading an Action Hero to Perform Like a Researcher (Action Hero language is *italicized*, Researcher language is **bold**.)

- Begin with praise in the preferred stage: "I am glad you are ready to *jump in* and *seize* this *opportunity*."
- Continue with mixing trigger language for the new task: "I don't want the project to stall or fail for lack of **preparation**. Please **research** the **information** we will need to be successful with this *opportunity*."

Persuading an Action Hero to perform like a Judge (Action Hero language is *italicized*, Judge language is **bold**.)

- Begin with praise in the preferred stage: "Your *foresight* to do this *now* will save us money."
- Continue with mixing trigger language for the new task: "Please **prioritize** the steps for the project and **why** each is necessary. Then we can receive approval to *get started* before the *opportunity* is past."

Sometimes the issue is convincing someone to stop doing the process he is highly motivated to continue. While this can be challenging depending on the individual, you will need to find a secondary motivator to stop him. Most individuals have a strong enough secondary area on the Wheel of Action Motivation to convince them to pause or cease for the success of the entire initiative. Use the following suggestions as a guide.

Convincing a Researcher to Stop Gathering Information. (The words to convince them to stop are **bold**.)

- Value and mission (Intention) as the secondary motivator to stop a Researcher: "For project success, it is **important** to stop gathering information and move to **evaluating** how the project fits with the **mission** and **values** of the company."

- Time and future success (Commitment) as the secondary motivator to stop a Researcher: "We must cease finding more information or we will never make the **deadlines** to reach our **goals**."

Convincing a Judge to stop deliberating or to be flexible. (The words to convince them to stop are **bold**.)

- Information and options (Attention) as the secondary motivator to stop a Judge: "Since the **information** we've found supports your position and **no other viable options** have been **discovered**, we should stop evaluating this decision."
- Time and future success (Commitment) as the secondary motivator to stop a Judge: "Our **deadline** is soon. Therefore, it is **time** to bring deliberation to a close, vote on whether to proceed and **make a viable plan**."

Convincing an Action Hero to stop planning or to look before leaping. (The words to convince them to stop are **bold**.)

- Value and mission (Intention) as the secondary motivator to stop an Action Hero: "The opportunity appears to be amazing. Before we go ahead, let's revisit the **company mission and goals** to make sure it is **in-line**."
- Information and options (Attention) as the secondary motivator to stop an Action Hero: "Since you have anticipated what could go wrong with the project plan, please **seek out** some **information** and client reviews to see if others have had the same issues before we start."

CHAPTER 16
Honestly Recognizing Conflict

Sometimes motivation and persuasion are not successful or tension remains despite the language techniques employed. In these instances, leaders find success by honestly recognizing the conflict or issue. Teams who have their Movement Pattern Analysis Profiles will often start tackling conflict from a place of identification because they understand the individual preferences of their teammates and can predict areas of conflict before they occur. Foreseeing conflict saves the team time and energy. Another bonus to the Movement Pattern Analysis Profile is its objectivity. Since the assessment is unbiased, the team can remain objective and take comments less personally.

When labeling conflict without analyst-created profile assessments to support your conversation, remain as unbiased as you can and be flexible. Your analysis may have some inaccuracies. Furthermore, human nature makes all comments personal and walls go up faster than they come down. Make conscious effort to remain open to continuing discussion about the problem. The leader will need to initially accept blame for the disagreement. The two of you work differently. Neither of you is doing something "wrong."

The following conversations which state problems honestly are not necessarily including Interaction Style. This can easily be added with statements such as, "I will work best with your opinion on this matter before I proceed." (Sharer); or "I will be more efficient and helpful to you with some time to work independently before responding to your question." (Private).

Examples of honest discussion:

A Researcher Talking to an Action Hero: "I'm going to be honest. This is not intended as criticism. Our working styles are simply different. By stating my concerns we can ease any tensions we may be feeling in our working relationship. I am feeling pushed by your quick timeline and worry that we will be entering this project without being fully prepared. Please read the information I sent to you and give me until the end of the week to send you the rest."

Or: "Changing the pace of the project and its deadlines is making it difficult for me to give you the information you need to be successful. I'm not coming from a place of criticism or blame, I simply work better with a timeline that is more constant. I don't want the project to fail because I wasn't able to give the team enough information at the right times."

A Researcher Talking to a Judge: "There is growing tension as we work on this project. I would like to share how I am feeling without blame to continue in a positive relationship. I fear your steadfastness on this issue, despite the information I've given you, may be harmful to the project long term. Please share with me why you remain strong on this issue. I would like to have an understanding and see it from your point of view."

Or: "I appreciate how you have categorized and prioritized the information I have given you. Our different working styles are beginning to clash a bit. There is some research that isn't clearly a positive or a negative but, in my opinion, should still be considered. I am asking a bit of flexibility from you to include the gray area information at the meeting as we deliberate on the issues."

A Judge talking to a Researcher: "To help me with the clarity I need to deliberate project viability in the CIO meeting, my presentation slides will list your information by priority followed by positives and negatives for each. The information laid out in this way will be easier for me. I am not changing any of your content. I don't want there to be unnecessary tension when my presentation looks different from what you sent me."

Or: "For me to make the strongest case for this project in the CIO meeting, I need to coalesce your information and only take in what is most substantiated. This is for the success of the project, not some way of discounting your research. I will have everything with me in case we are asked something not anticipated, but the boss will be overwhelmed with too much information."

A Judge Talking to an Action Hero: "I sense our differing work styles are starting to show! I am not comfortable moving ahead without consensus on more details of the project. One more team meeting to ensure this is the correct action will make implementation much easier. I don't feel we have the support from everyone we need to make this a success."

Or: "I feel some of the consequences you are bringing to our attention are unwarranted based on the information that has been gathered. I know the completion of the project by deadline is important to you. I'm suggesting you wait to alert us to possible consequences as they arise, so we can move ahead and decide the merit of the project during the quarterly meeting."

An Action Hero Talking to a Researcher: "I understand your need to be fully prepared, and I value the information to prevent surprises. However, I feel we are prepared and the timing for this opportunity is fading quickly. My style is to research specifics as we go along, therefore I am starting to feel tension in our working relationship because the process is being slowed."

Or: "I realize there may be more options out there if we look further. However, I feel you have found a very viable option that will serve us well and fix our current problem. The urgency I feel to implement your solution is causing much stress on our relationship and is negatively affecting the team."

An Action Hero Talking to a Judge: "I know I can get caught up in how amazing this opportunity is for our company and you are doing the right thing by evaluating its merit. However, I feel pressure from the magnitude of the plan we have created and feel strongly of our need to begin. Please help me understand what reservations remain which are preventing your approval of the project."

Or: "I have heard all the deliberation on this initiative and need to understand why there is concern over whether or not it fits the company mission. I would like to resolve the tension between us before it hampers our working relationship. I feel time is against us being able to complete the project because we have not begun."

You may be wondering why budget discussions are missing from the conversation examples. The decision-making process can be influenced by money, but it depends on the person. Money may not be a motivator or it may not be relevant to the project. If budget is a concern, add to persuasion as in the examples below. Be warned, however, that you should examine whether your colleague is motivated by money or not. The cause for tension may be that you place a high importance on sticking to budget and your colleague values something else. Including the budget in your discussion may cause tension to escalate higher and provoke a response like, "You always bring up the budget!" or "This is not about money!" It is also easy to fall into the trap of placing all the blame of your difficult relationship on money alone. While challenging, keep the conversation as neutral as possible.

Money added to some of the honest discussion examples (money language is in *italics*):

A Researcher Talking to an Action Hero: "I'm going to be honest. This is not intended as criticism. Our working styles are simply different. By stating my concerns we can ease any tensions we may be feeling in our working relationship. I am feeling pushed by your quick timeline and worry that we will be entering this project without being fully prepared. *It is my understanding we cannot go over budget on this item. Unknown costs and lack of research into the cost will put the budget at risk.* Please read the information I sent to you and give me until the end of the week to *compile costs* on the rest."

A Researcher Talking to a Judge: "There is growing tension as we work on this project. I would like to share how I am feeling without blame. It is all for the success of our relationship. I fear your steadfastness on the *issue of budget*, despite the information I've given you on how it is impossible to complete this project *inexpensively. Cutting corners now will be harmful to the company long term.* Please share with me *why you remain unwilling to look creatively at finding more money* so that I can have understanding and see it from your point of view."

A Judge Talking to a Researcher: "For me to make the strongest case for this project in the CIO meeting, I need to coalesce your information and only share what is most substantiated. *This is especially important when discussing budget numbers.* I do this for the success of the project, not some way of discounting your research. I will take everything we have into the meeting in case we are asked for something not anticipated, but the boss will be overwhelmed with too much."

A Judge Talking to an Action Hero: "I sense our differing work styles are starting to show! I am not comfortable moving ahead without consensus on more details of the project *like the budget.* One more team meeting to ensure this is the correct action *within the budget restraints* will make implementation much easier. I don't feel we have support from everyone we need to make this a success."

An Action Hero Talking to a Researcher: "I understand your need to be fully prepared, and I value the information to prevent surprises. However, I feel we are prepared and the timing for this opportunity is fading quickly. *The price we were given will only be held for one more day.* My style is to research specifics as we go along, therefore I am starting to feel tension in our working relationship because the process is being slowed."

An Action Hero Talking to a Judge: "I know I can get caught up in how amazing this opportunity is for our company and you are doing the right thing by evaluating its merit *within our budgetary constraints.* However, I feel pressure from the magnitude of the plan we have created and the need to begin is great. *The prices of our materials are more likely to rise than* *lower.* Please help me understand what reservations remain which are preventing your go ahead on the project."

CHAPTER 17
Customer Relations

Customers or clients create a team relationship with its own dynamic. Do not forget to consider the customer and their preferences when utilizing the information in this book. All of the tips and tools can be extremely helpful when interacting with individuals outside of the company. Create intake surveys for your customers.

Some particular considerations:

Match Decision-Making Style preferences of sales reps with customers. Do your best to determine some basic decision-making styles of your customers and match them to reps with similar styles. Do not be afraid to switch sales reps if a customer relationship is fraught with tension. If territories are specific it may not be possible, but the sales department will be more successful if Researchers are matched with Researchers for example. The sales rep will already be more inclined to speak the language the customer wants and needs to hear, thereby increasing the likelihood of a sale and repeat business. The Researcher sales representative will not be annoyed by giving a client extra details that an Action Hero sales representative would consider unnecessary.

Match Interaction Style preferences of sales reps with customers. Similar to matching decision-making preference, pairing Interaction Styles can also smooth sales interactions. The Sharing customer will not annoy a Sharing sales rep with multiple calls and e-mails. Match Neutral and Versatile sales reps with Private customers and vice versa, as they can relate to a Private without complete lack of communication which may occur when two Privates are together.

Frame sales conversations to match the client's preference. If sales reps are not matched to client decision-making style, they can be taught to use motivational trigger language (see the chapter on Motivational Language). The same piece of information can be framed with trigger language to motivate the buyer.

An example:

Selling advertising to a Researcher: *"This page **lists the information** for the **type** of ads in this package both in print and on the web. They run on…."*

Selling advertising to a Judge: *"This page will **clarify** for you the number of ads in this package both in print and on the web. This is one place where we are often **superior** to other firms because…"*

Selling advertising to an Action Hero: *"This page will illuminate our **process** with advertising. Our **goal** is to give you the most exposure to your target market for your…"*

Recognize Decision-Making Style and Interaction Style preferences for conflict resolution. If a customer is irate, utilize all the tools for verbal communication and recognizing conflict. Calming an upset individual will be faster and easier if you can quickly determine where the communication or problem occurred. In conflict resolution, the overall habits of the customer do not matter as much as the customer's immediate process issue.

Does the customer feel he is ill-informed or is not given enough information? Respond as if he is a Researcher. Is the customer being inflexible? Treat him like a Judge. Is the issue with installation or follow through? Consider the customer an Action Hero. You may have an idea of the customer's Interaction Preference as well. If he is upset about ignored

communication, for example, the issue may be a Sharing client
with a Private sales representative.

CHAPTER 18
Take a Bow!

Congratulations!

"The wheel is come full circle."
William Shakespeare, *King Lear*

The information in this book is very detailed and you have read to the end! The exercises, dialogues and graphics in the book are to support you as you make sense of it all. The information is too valuable and business-changing to keep behind the curtain.

Awareness of the different types of decision-making styles has a large impact on employee relationships and company morale. The tools and tips in the book are meant to encourage tolerance and patience which are often in short supply. Please encourage others in your organization to read the book.

Finally, this book is truly not complete without your personal Movement Pattern Analysis Profile to know definitively where you fall on the Wheel of Action Motivations. Call Moving Image and let us address your business communication needs. Take this information and grow more than you even imagine.

I applaud you. The standing ovation begins now...

About Alison Henderson

Alison Henderson, MFA, GL-CMA, MPACC, is a business owner, artistic director and acting coach with a passion for discovering the intrinsic motivations of her clients. Whether propelling a business or an acting career, Alison is a master at improving communication to make the greatest impact on your audience.

Having feet firmly planted in both business and theater for most of her life, Moving Image Consulting was founded to use all of Alison's skills and to share her knowledge of non-verbal behavior and its connection to the decision-making process. There are only 22 Movement Pattern Analysts in the world. Alison is committed to sharing this unique technique and praising its virtues. Whether an executive reaching new heights or an actor improving his craft, Alison is committed to serving them all.

Connect with Alison at:
www.movingimageconsulting.com
www.facebook.com/movingimageconsulting
@SpiralMovingAH

My Notes:

My Notes:

_____

_____

_____

_____

_____

_____

_____

_____

_____

_____

_____

_____

_____

_____

_____

_____

www.ingramcontent.com/pod-product-compliance
Lightning Source LLC
Chambersburg PA
CBHW070821180526
45168CB00002B/707